Welcome — page 6

Colors		Relationship skills
black, blue, brown, green, orange, pink, purple, red, white, yellow	Hello / Hi / Welcome, class!; Goodbye Hi, I'm (name).	Welcoming new people to class

	Vocabulary	Grammar and communication	Story	Personal and Social Skills	Cross-curricular
6 Nature page 60	**Bugs** ant, beetle, butterfly, ladybug **Nature** flower, mushroom, pond, river, rock, tree	I can see a beetle. **Asking and answering about nature** What color is it? It's red.	**A good team** Help me! It's a team.	**Social awareness:** Teamwork Let's all help. Good idea!	**Math and art:** Symmetry spots, stripes
7 Food page 70	**Food 1** apples, cake, soup, tea **Food 2** cookies, ice cream, juice, noodles, pizza, sandwiches	I like pizza. **Talking about likes and dislikes** I like soup. I don't like noodles.	**Lunch for Cam** hungry, lunchbox; Thanks.	**Self-management:** Empathy nice I can help. Let's all share. Thank you.	**Art:** Food prints bell pepper, mushroom, onion; cut, paint
8 Animals page 80	**Animals** bird, elephant, lion, monkey, zebra **Actions 2** climb, fly, run, swim, walk	I can swim. **Describing animal abilities** Monkeys can climb.	**Sports day** glasses, hero, shoes; Now I can run. Here you are.	**Self-awareness:** Asking for help I can do it. I need help.	**Science:** Animal needs food, home, water
9 In the city page 90	**City** car, house, street, train **Adjectives** fast, long, new, old, short, slow	It's a fast car. **Describing things in the city** It's a train. It's very fast.	**A school trip** snake; Are you OK? Be nice!	**Self-awareness:** Being brave That's brave. I'm very brave.	**Social Science:** Road safety Go. Look left/right. Stop. Wait.

Say hello!

1  Listen, sing, and act. .TPR

2  Listen, point, and say.

My **Disney**

STARS AND HEROES

S

STARTER

Student's Book with eBook

Amanda Davies

Scope and Sequence

	Vocabulary	Grammar and communication	Story	Personal and Social Skills	Cross-curricular
1 My family page 10 	**Family** brother, dad, mom, sister **Numbers 1** one, two, three, four, five, six	I'm six. Are you five? Yes./No. **Asking and answering about family** Who's this? This is my brother.	**A new friend** friend, happy, sad; Oh no!	 **Self-awareness:** Identifying my emotions 1 happy, sad Are you happy? I'm sad.	**Science:** Shadows cloudy, shadows, sunny
2 My room page 20 	**Room** bed, chair, desk, poster **Toys** ball, kite, puppet, scooter, teddy bear, yo-yo	It's a ball. It's small. **Asking and answering about toys** Is it a kite? Yes. It's a kite.	**The puppet show** Let's play!	**Self-awareness:** Identifying my emotions 2 grumpy I'm not grumpy. Let's play!	**Math:** Shapes circle, rectangle, triangle
3 My school page 30	**School items** backpack, book, crayon, marker, pencil, ruler **Numbers 2** seven, eight, nine, ten	I have two rulers. **Asking and answering about objects** How many books? I have one book.	**The surprise** surprise, tortoise; Wow!	**Self-awareness:** Identifying my emotions 3 nervous I'm not nervous. It's OK. Don't worry.	**Math:** Plus and minus is, minus, plus
4 My body page 40 	**Body** arm, body, hand, head, leg, nose **Actions 1** clap, shake, stomp, touch	Stomp your feet. Don't move. **Asking and answering about the body** What's this? It's my nose.	**Fun with Shelly** I have an idea. I'm excited! Yippee!	**Self-awareness:** Expressing my emotions cry, excited, jump, smile I'm happy. I smile.	**Technology:** Coding up, down, left, right; Go left!
5 My clothes page 50 	**Clothes 1** pants, shoes, skirt, socks **Clothes 2** coat, dress, hat, scarf, sweater, T-shirt	My coat is red. **Talking about clothes** I'm wearing my T-shirt.	**The yo-yo** Come and play!	**Self-management:** Persistence Good job! Keep trying!	**Technology:** Materials cotton, leather, wool

3 ✏️ Be a hero. Draw.

Name:

4 Collect your friends!

 Welcome!

1 0.3 Listen, point, and say. Then play. **TPR**

2 OA Watch. Color and say.

black, blue, brown, green, orange, pink, purple, red, white, yellow

3 Find and stick. Then circle who's in the video.

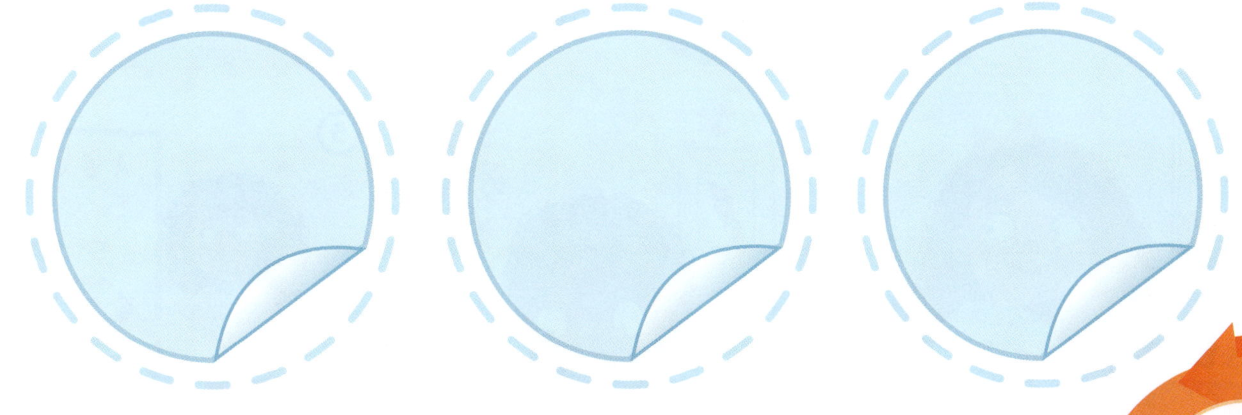

4 Listen and say.

5 Listen, chant, and act. TPR

goodbye, hello, hi; I'm (name).

1 Find and say.

2 🎧 0.6 Listen and point.

Hello, Class!

Say *hello.*

3 ✏️ 💬 **Match and say the names.**

4 💬 **Act out the story.**

5 🎵 **Listen, sing, and act.** TPR 🎵 *goodbye, goodbye* 🎵

Hello, goodbye, I'm (name); class, welcome

1 My family

1 Watch. Who's in the video? Check (✔).

2 Circle for Merida.

3 Listen, find, and say. Then play.

4 Listen, chant, and act. TPR

Go to page 4

brother, dad, mom, sister

1  Listen, point, and stick. Then play.

2  Listen and show. Then play.

3 Count, clap, and say. **TPR**

one, two, three, four, five, six

Sing-along

1 🎵 1.5 **Listen and point. Then sing and act.** TPR

2 🎧 1.6 💬 **Listen and find. Then ask and answer.**

3 🎧 1.7 💬 **Listen and color. Then play.**

Song: I'm (six). Are you (five)? Yes./No.

A new friend

1  Listen to the story. Point to  .

2 🎧 1.9 ✏️ **Who says it? Listen, circle, and say.**

① ② ③

3 **Look and draw** 🙂 **or** 🙁**.**

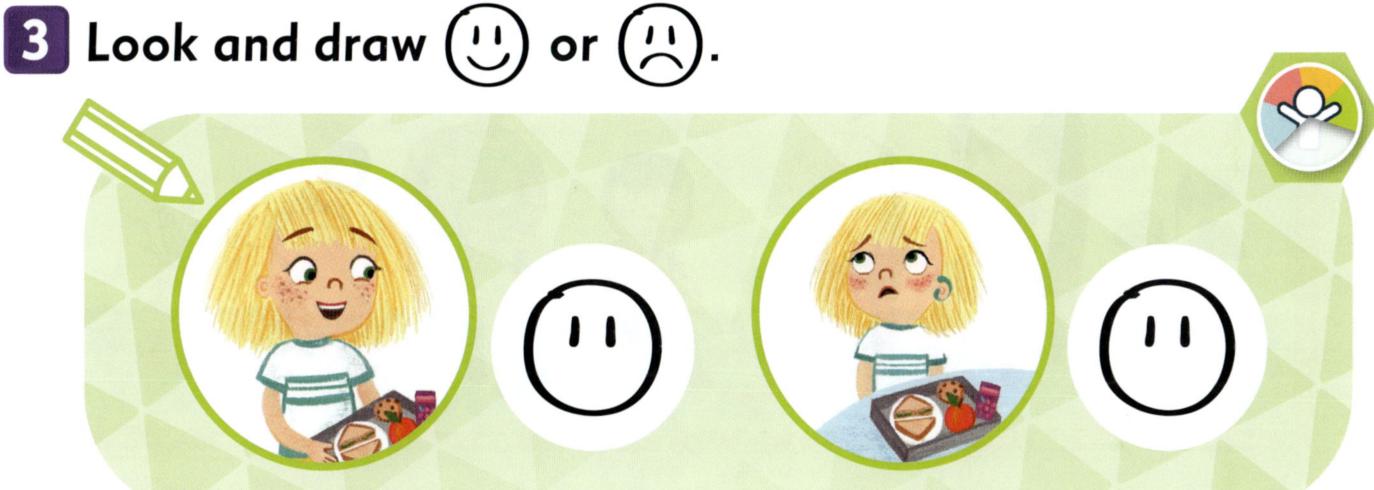

4 💬 **Act out the story.**

1   Watch. Who gives a ? Circle.

2   Listen and find. Then ask and answer.

3 Listen and say. Then make and play.

Skills: Who's this? This is my (brother).

Extra Lesson

Happy and sad

1  Listen and point. Then say. *(1.13)*

2 Draw 🙂 or 🙁 for you. Then ask and answer.

3 Make your friend happy. Act and say. **TPR**

Shadows

1 🎧 1.14 **Listen and point. Then say.**

2 💬 ✏️ **Say *sunny* or *cloudy*. Then circle the shadows.**

3 ✏️ **Look and match.**

Shadows: cloudy, shadows, sunny

I can do it!

1  Play and say.

2 Think and color. Then stick!

2 My room

1 Watch. Who has a ? Point.

2 Circle for Mike.

3 Listen, find, and say. Then play.

4 Listen, chant, and act. TPR

4

Go to page 4

bed, chair, desk, poster

1 Listen, point, and say. Then play.

2 Look, stick, and say. Then listen and check.

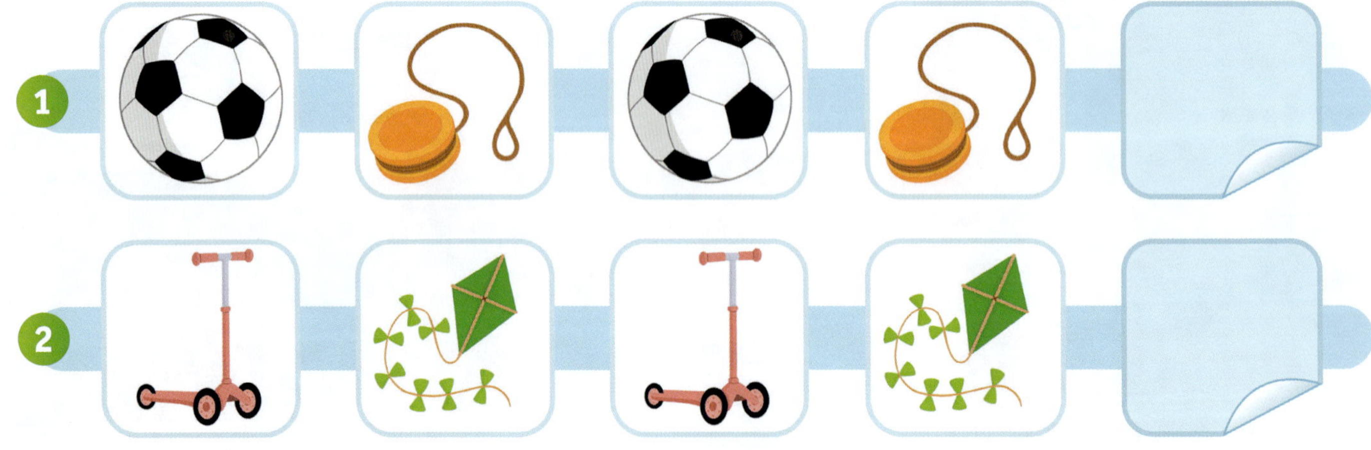

3 Draw. Then say and act. **TPR**

ball, kite, puppet, scooter, teddy bear, yo-yo

Sing-along

1 🎵 2.5 **Listen and point. Then sing and act.** ·TPR

2 🎧 2.6 💬 **Listen and find. Then say.**

3 ✏️ 💬 **Color. Then point and say.**

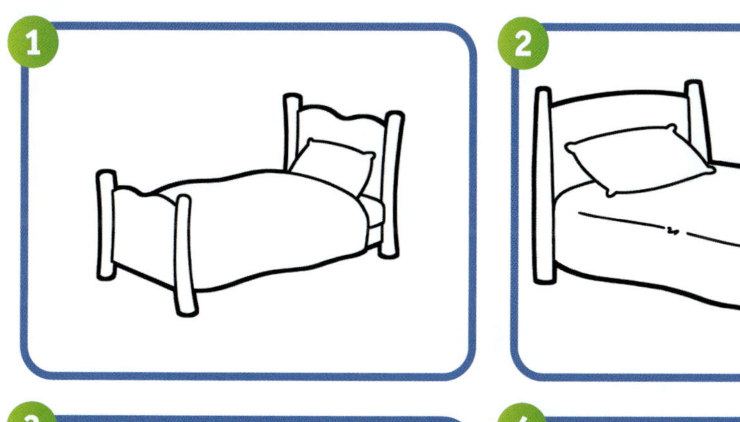

Song: It's a (ball). It's (small/red).

The puppet show

1  Listen to the story. Who has a 🌽?

2  Who says it? Listen and point. Then say.

3  Look and match. Then listen and say.

4 Act out the story.

1 ▶ Watch. Check (✔) the bed.

2 🎧 2.10 ✏️ Listen and circle. Then ask and answer.

3 🎧 2.11 💬 Listen and point. Then make and play.

Skills: Is it a (kite)? Yes. It's a (kite).

>>> **Extra Lesson** >>>>>>>

Go online
Phonics

I'm not grumpy

1  2.12 Check (✔)  . Then listen, point, and say.

2 2.13 Listen and circle. Then act and say for you.

 1 

2  

3 2.14 Listen and check (✔). Then say.

1  2 

Shapes

1 🎧 2.15 **Listen and point. Then say.**

1 

2 

3 

2 💬 ✏️ **Find and say. Then trace and circle.**

2   4

2   5

1   4

3 💬 **Make a shape monster. Then point and say.**

Shapes: circle, rectangle, triangle

I can do it!

1 Play and say.

2 Think and color. Then stick!

I can ...

1

2

3

✓ Unit 2!

Go online
Big Project

3 My school

1 Watch. Who's in school? Check (✔).

2  **Circle for Bonnie.**

3 **Listen, point, and say. Then play.**

1  2  3  4  5  6 

4 **Listen, chant, and act.** TPR 

Go to page 4

backpack, book, crayon, marker, pencil, ruler

1  Listen, point, and say. Then play.

2 Listen and color. Then count and say.

a 

b 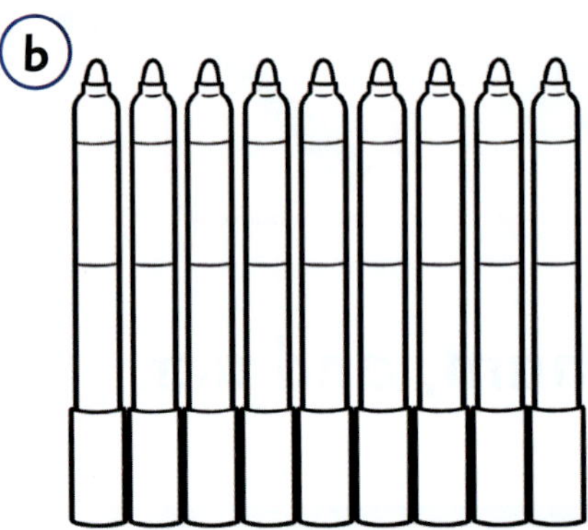

c 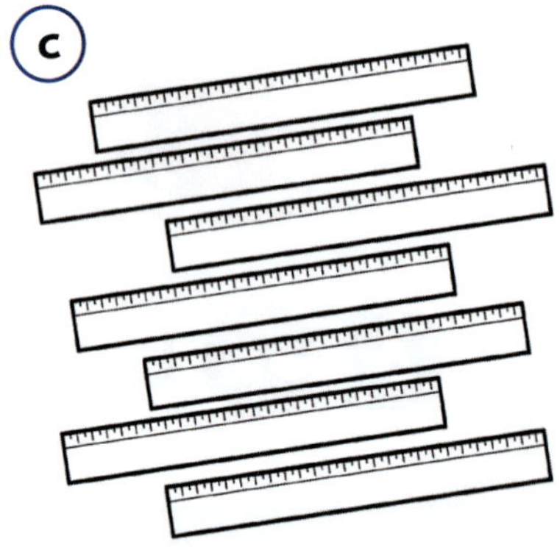

3 Find 📗 , 🎒 , and ✏️ . Count and say.

seven, eight, nine, ten

Sing-along

1 🎵 3.5 **Listen and point. Then sing and act.** TPR

2 🎧 3.6 💬 **Listen and find. Then say.**

3 ✏️ 💬 **Draw. Then ask and answer.**

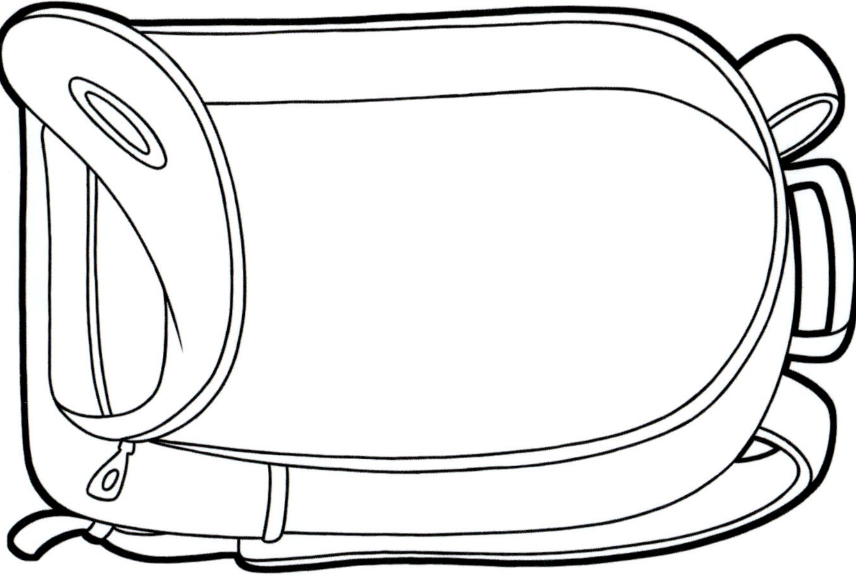

Song: I have (two) (rulers).

The surprise

1  3.7 Listen to the story. Is 🐢 6, 7, or 8?

3 **Who's nervous? Circle.**

4 **Act out the story.**

Story: surprise, tortoise; Wow!

1 Watch and check (✔).

1

2

2 Listen and stick. Then ask and answer.

1

2

3 Listen and point. Then make and play.

Skills: How many (books)? I have (one) (book).

Extra Lesson

Go online
Phonics

I'm nervous

1 Who's nervous? Check (✔). Then say.

1.12 Listen and sing.

2 3.11 Listen and point. Then act and say. **TPR**

3 Look and colour for you. Then say.

Self-awareness: I'm (not) nervous. It's OK. Don't worry.

Plus and minus

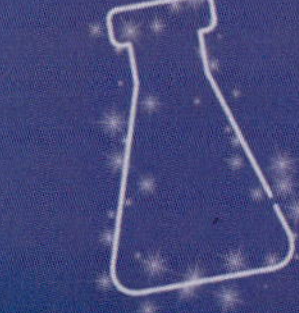

---

1 Listen and point. Then show and say. **TPR** (3.12)

①  ②  ③ 

---

2 Listen and draw. Then point and say. (3.13)

①

$2 \quad \bigcirc \quad 3 \quad = \quad 5$

②

$5 \quad \bigcirc \quad 4 \quad = \quad 9$

③

$7 \quad \bigcirc \quad 1 \quad = \quad 6$

---

3 Make equations. Then test your friend.

Math: is, minus, plus

I can do it!

1 💬 Play and say.

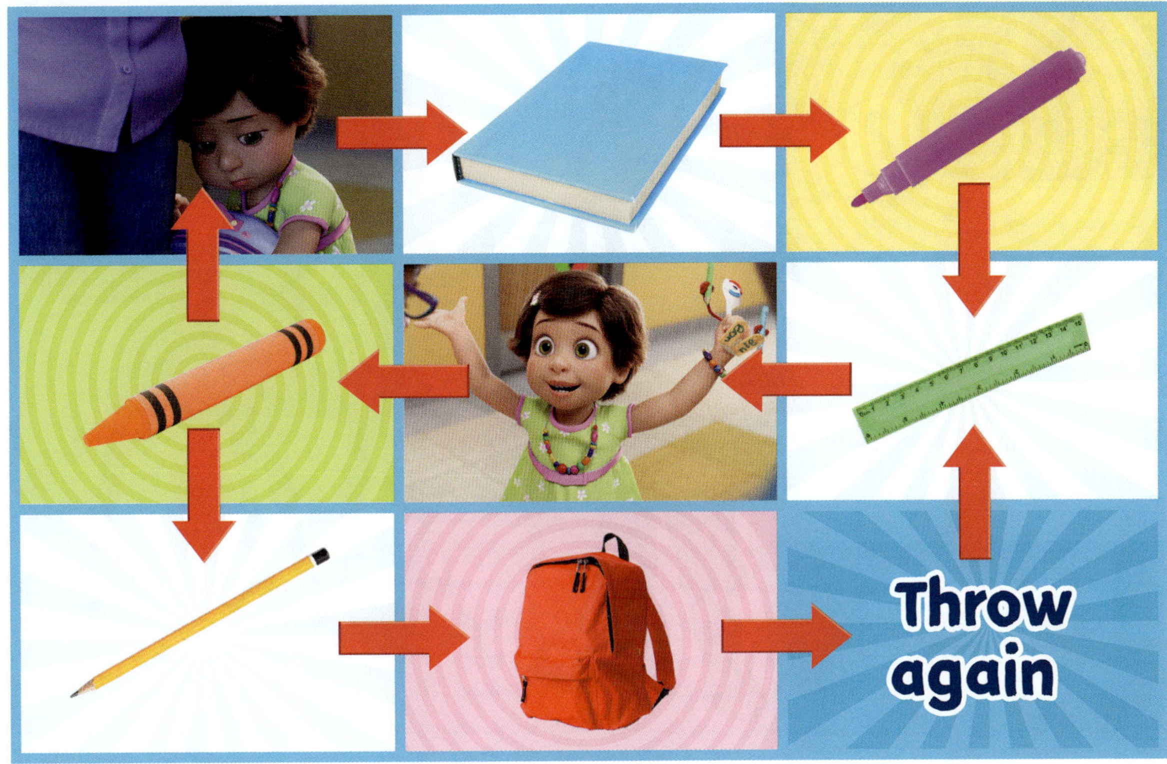

2 💡✏️ Think and color. Then stick!

I can ...

1

2

3

✔️ Unit 3!

4 My body

1  Watch. Who's in ? Check (✔).

2 Circle for Anna.

3 Listen, find, and say. Then count.

4 Listen, chant, and act. TPR

Go to page 4

arm, body, hand, head, leg, nose

1 **Listen, point, and say. Then play.** _4.3_

 1

 2

 3

 4

2 **Listen and stick. Then say.** _4.4_

1   

2   

3 **Listen and do. Then play.** TPR _4.5_

clap, shake, stomp, touch

Sing-along

1 Listen and point. Then sing and act. **TPR**

2 Listen and do. Then say.

3 Listen and do. Then play. **TPR**

Elsa says ...

Song: Stomp your feet. Don't (move).

Fun with Shelly

1 Listen to the story. Point to  .

2 4.10 Who says it? Listen and point. Then say.

3 Look and match. Then show and say.

4 Act out the story.

Story: I have an idea. I'm excited! Yippee!

Grammar and Speaking

1   Watch. Who's in the video? Circle.

2   Listen and trace. Then ask and answer.

3 Listen and point. Then make and play.

Skills: What's this? It's my (nose).

Extra Lesson >>>>>>>>>>>

Go online
Phonics

Feelings and my body

1 4.13 **Listen and point. Then say and act.** TPR

1.12
Listen and sing.

2 **Look, act and say.** TPR

3 4.14 **Listen and make an "I'm excited" dance.** TPR

Self-awareness: cry, excited, jump, smile; I'm (happy). I (smile).

Coding

1  Listen and trace. Then say and act. **TPR**

2 Help Sven. Count. Then listen and check (✔).

3 Help Shelly. Draw. Then tell a friend.

Coding: up, down, left, right; go (left)!

I can do it!

1   **Play. Say and draw O or X.**

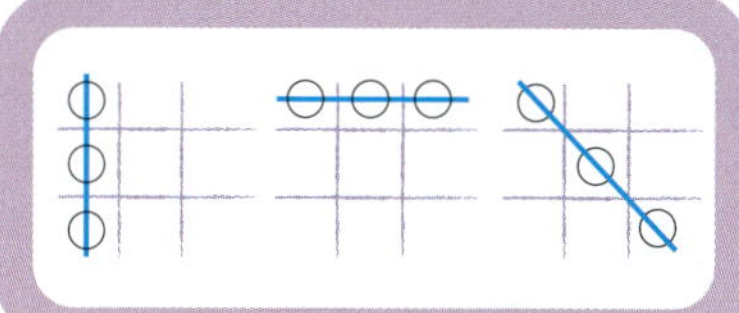

 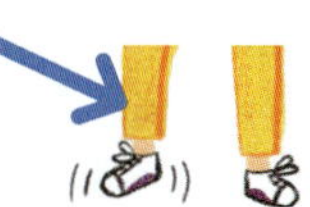  

2   **Think and color. Then stick!**

I can ...

 1 

2

 3

✓ **Unit 4!**

5 My clothes
1 skirt
2 shoes
3 socks
4 pants

1 ▶ Watch. Who's in the video? Check (✔).

2 ▶ Who keeps trying? Circle.

3 🎧 💬 Listen, find, and say. Then play.

4 🎵 Listen, chant, and act. **.TPR**

1 🎧 5.3 💬 **Listen, point, and say. Then play.**

2 🎧 5.4 💬 **Listen and stick. Then say.**

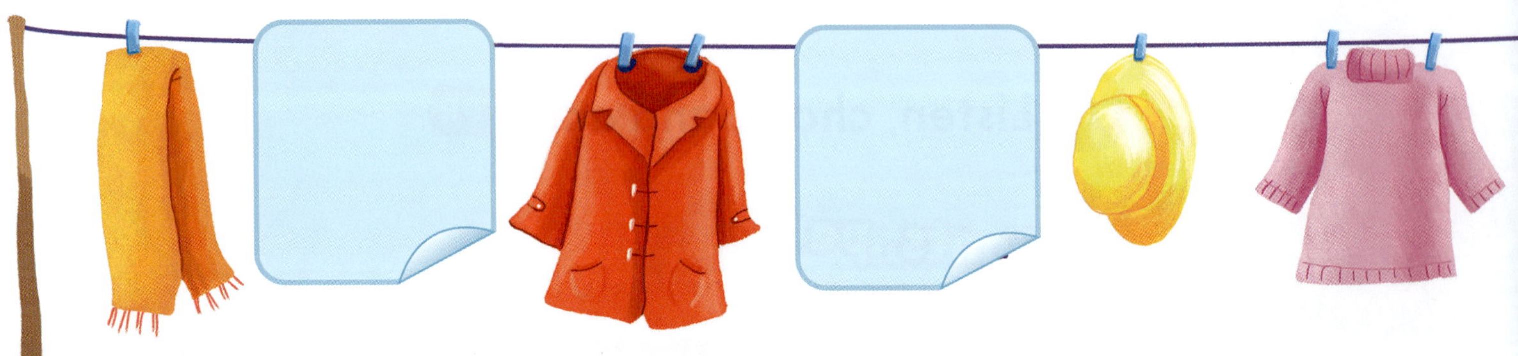

3 💬 🎧 5.5 **Look and guess. Then listen and check.**

coat, dress, hat, scarf, sweater, T-shirt

Sing-along

1 🎵 5.6 **Listen and point. Then sing and act.** TPR

2 🎧 5.7 **Listen and say *Peter* or *Maya*. Then play.**

3 ✏️ 💬 **Draw. Then compare with a friend.**

Song: My (coat) is (red).

The yo-yo

1  Listen to the story. Who's  ?

 Who says it? Listen and point. Then say.

3 **Who keeps trying? Look and circle.**

4 **Act out the story.**

Grammar and Speaking

1   Watch. Who's wearing a 👗? Circle.

2  Listen and color. Then say for you.

1 

2 

3 

3 Listen and point. Then make and play.

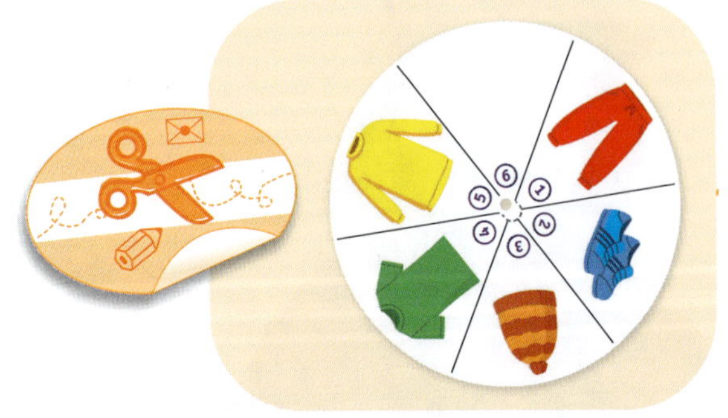  

Skills: I'm wearing my (T-shirt). | Extra Lesson ⟩⟩⟩⟩⟩ | Go online Phonics

Keep trying!

1 🎧 5.12 💬 **Listen and point. Then say.**

2 💬 **Look and say.**

3 💬 **Look and do. Then say.** TPR

Materials

1 🎧 5.13 Listen and point. Then say.

1 cotton

2 wool

3 leather

2 ✏️ 🎧 5.14 Match. Listen and check. Then say.

1

2

3

a

b

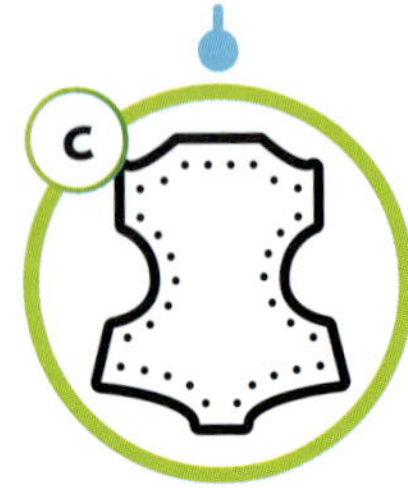
c

3 ✏️ 💬 Draw clothes. Then say.

Materials: cotton, leather, wool

I can do it!

1 Say and point. Then trace.

hat

socks

pants

shoes

2 Think and color. Then stick!

I can ...

1

3

2

☑ Unit 5!

6 Nature

1 6A ✏️ **Watch. What do the ants make? Circle.**

2 **6A** Check (✔) the team.

3 **6.1** Listen, point, and say. Then play.

1 ant

2 beetle

3 butterfly

4 ladybug

4 **6.2** Listen, chant, and act. TPR

Go to
page 5

1 🎧 6.3 💬 **Listen, point, and say. Then play.**

2 🎧 6.4 💬 **Listen, point, and stick. Then say.**

3 🎧 6.5 💬 **Listen and find. Then play.**

flower, mushroom, pond, river, rock, tree

Sing-along

1 ♪ *6.6* **Listen and color. Then sing and act.** .TPR

2 *6.7* 💬 **Listen and find. Then say.**

3 💬 **Guess, point, and say.**

1

2

3

4

5

6

A good team

1 🎧 6.8 **Listen to the story. Point to a** **, a** **, and a** **.**

  **Listen and point. Then say.**

3 **Who's the team? Circle.**

4 **Act out the story.**

Story: Help me! It's a team.

1  6B  **Watch. Who's Dot? Circle.**

2 6.10 **Listen and check (✔). Then ask and answer.**

3 6.11 **Listen and point. Then make and play.**

Skills: What color is it? It's (red).

Extra Lesson

Teamwork

1 Look and circle good teamwork.

2 6.12 Listen and point. Then say and act. .TPR

3 Work in groups. Make "TEAM." .TPR

  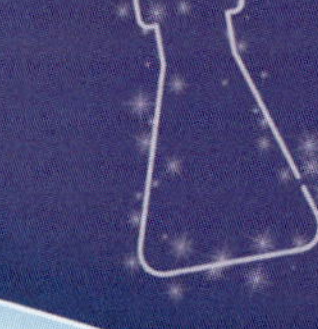

Symmetry

1  6.13  **Listen and point. Then find and say.**

2  **Look and match. Then say.**

3   **Draw and color. Then say.**

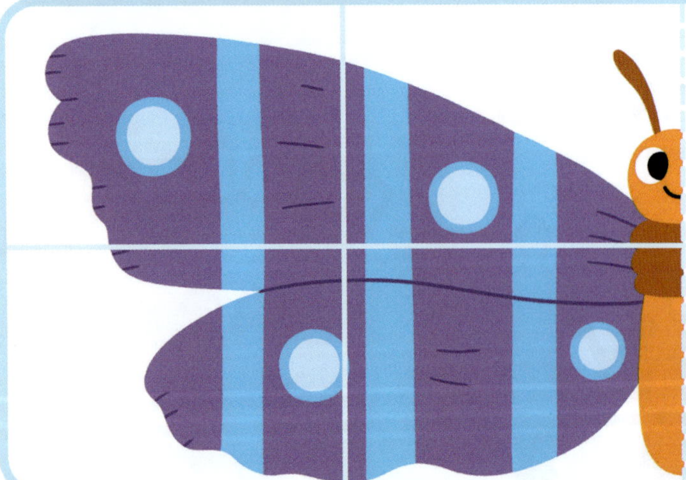

Symmetry: spots, stripes

I can do it!

1  Say and point. Then trace.

tree

ant

rock   pond   beetle ladybug

2 6.14 Listen and find. Then play.

3 Think and color. Then stick!

I can ...

7 Food

1 7A Watch. Who has a 👕? Point.

2 7A Who's nice? Circle.

3 7.1 Listen, find, and say. Then play.

4 7.2 Listen, chant, and act. **TPR** ♪ soup, soup ♪

apples, cake, soup, tea

1 7.3 Listen, point, and say. Then play.

2 7.4 Listen and check (✔). Then look and say.

3 Draw your lunch. Then say.

cookies, ice cream, juice, noodles, pizza, sandwiches

Sing-along

1 🎵 7.5 **Listen and point. Then sing and act.** TPR

2 🎧 7.6 💬 **Listen and find. Then play.**

3 💬 **Check (✔) what you like. Then say.**

Lunch for Cam

1  Listen to the story. Who likes  ?

   **Listen and number. Then say.**

3 **Who's nice? Circle.**

4 **Act out the story.**

Story: hungry, lunchbox; Thanks.

1 Watch. What does Belle like? Check (✔).

1 2 3

2 Listen, point, and stick. Then say for you.

3 Listen and point. Then make and play.

Skills: I like (soup). I don't like (noodles).

Extra Lesson

Be nice

1 Who are they nice to? Match.

2 7.11 Listen and point.

3 Choose and act. TPR

Food prints

1  7.12  **Listen and point. Then say.**

1 bell pepper

2 onion

3 cut

4 paint

2 7.13 **Look and match. Then listen and say.**

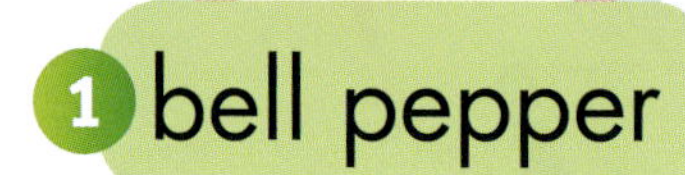
1

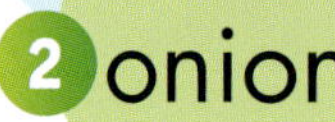
2

3

a

b

c

3 **Look and number in order. Then say.**

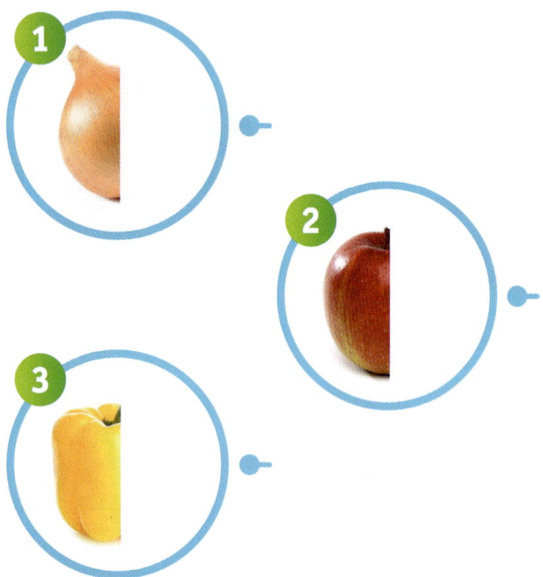
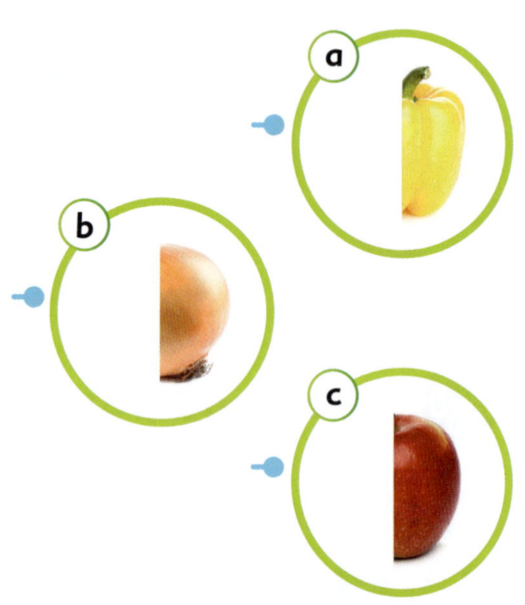

Food prints: bell pepper, mushroom, onion; cut, paint

I can do it!

1 🎧 7.14 ✏️ **Listen and color. Then trace.**

2 💬 **Draw 🙂 or 🙁 for you. Then say.**

3 💡 ✏️ **Think and color. Then stick!**

1 8A ✏️ Watch. Who jumps? Circle.

2 ▶ 8A Who asks for help? Check (✔).

3 🎧 8.1 💬 Listen, find, and say. Then play.

4 🎵 8.2 Listen, chant, and act. **TPR**

4 bird

5 monkey

Go to page 5

1 🎧 8.3 💬 **Listen, point, and say. Then play.**

1 run

2 fly

3 climb

4 walk

5 swim

2 🎧 8.4 ✏️ **Listen and number. Then point and say.**

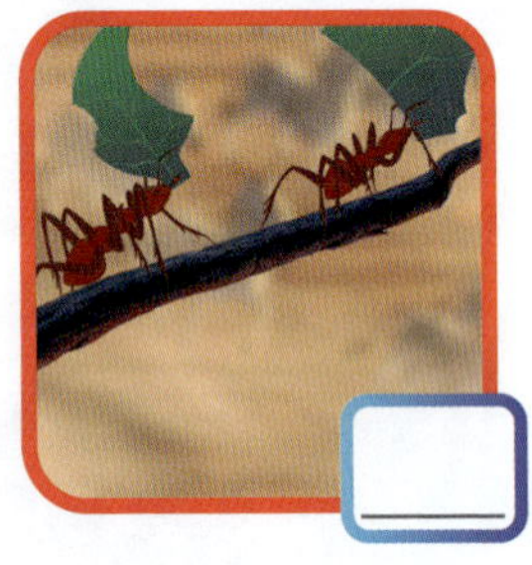

3 **Say and act.** TPR

climb, fly, run, swim, walk

Sing-along

1 (8.5) **Listen and point. Then sing and act.** TPR

2 (8.6) **Listen and find. Then say.**

3 (8.7) **Listen, point, and stick. Then say and guess.**

Song: I can (swim). I'm (small).

Sports day

1  Listen to the story. Who can ? Who can ?

2 Who says it? Listen, circle, and say.

① ② ③

3 Who needs help? Check (✔).

4 Act out the story.

1   Watch. Circle for Simba.

2  Match. Then listen, check, and say. **8.10**

a

b

c

3 Listen and say. Then make and play. **8.11**

Skills: (Monkeys) can (climb).

Extra Lesson

Go online
Phonics

Asking for help

1   **Listen and point. Then say.**

2 **Point and say.**

3 **Make a flip sign. Then play.**

Self-awareness: I can do it. I need help.

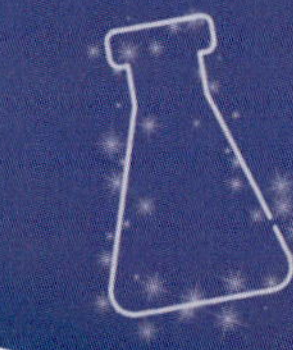

Animal needs

1   **Listen and point. Then say.**

8.13

3 Birds need food.

1 Birds need a home.

2 Birds need water.

2   **Circle for lions. Then say.**

3   **Draw for monkeys. Then say.**

Animal needs: food, home, water

I can do it!

1   **Choose, trace, and say.**

1 

run / fly

2
fly / climb

3
climb / walk

4  

fly / climb

2 **What can you do? Say.**

3 **Think and color. Then stick!**

I can ...

1

2

3

89

In the city

1 **9A** Watch. Circle Judy's hat.

2  Who's brave? Check (✔).

3 Listen, point, and say. Then play.

1 
street

2 
house

3 
car

4 
train

4 Listen, chant, and act. **TPR**

Go to page 5

car, house, street, train

1 9.3 Listen, point, and say. Then play.

2 9.4 Listen and put a ✔ or ✗. Then play.

3 Play. Say and guess.

fast, long, new, old, short, slow

Sing-along

1 🎵 (9.5) Listen, point, and stick. Then sing and act. **TPR**

2 🎧 (9.6) 💬 Listen and find. Then say.

3 💬 Look and find five differences. Then say.

Song: It's a (fast) (car).

A school trip

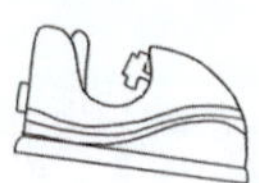

1  Listen to the story. Point to 🏠 and 🛹.

2  Listen and match.

3 Who's brave? Circle.

4 Act out the story.

Story: snake; Are you OK? Be nice!

Grammar and Speaking

1 Watch. What color is the 🛹? Check (✔).

2 Listen and number. Then play. (9.9)

3 Listen and point. Then make and play. (9.10)

Skills: It's a (train). It's very (fast).

Extra Lesson

Go online
Phonics

Being brave

1  Listen and point. Then say.

🎵 1.12
Listen and sing.

2 What do you do when you don't feel brave? Circle.

3 How do you feel? Color and tell a friend.

not brave	brave	very brave

Self-awareness: That's brave. I'm (very) brave.

Social Science

Road safety

1 🎧 9.12 💬 **Listen and point. Then say.**

1 Stop.

2 Go.

3 Wait.

5 Look left.

4 Look right.

2 🎧 9.13 ✏️ **Number in order. Then listen and check.**

☐ Go.

☐ Stop.

☐ Wait.

☐ Look.

3 ✏️ 💬 **Make. Then act.** TPR

Road safety: Go. Look left / right. Stop. Wait.

I can do it!

1 🖊 **Trace and write.**

long   old   slow   car   house

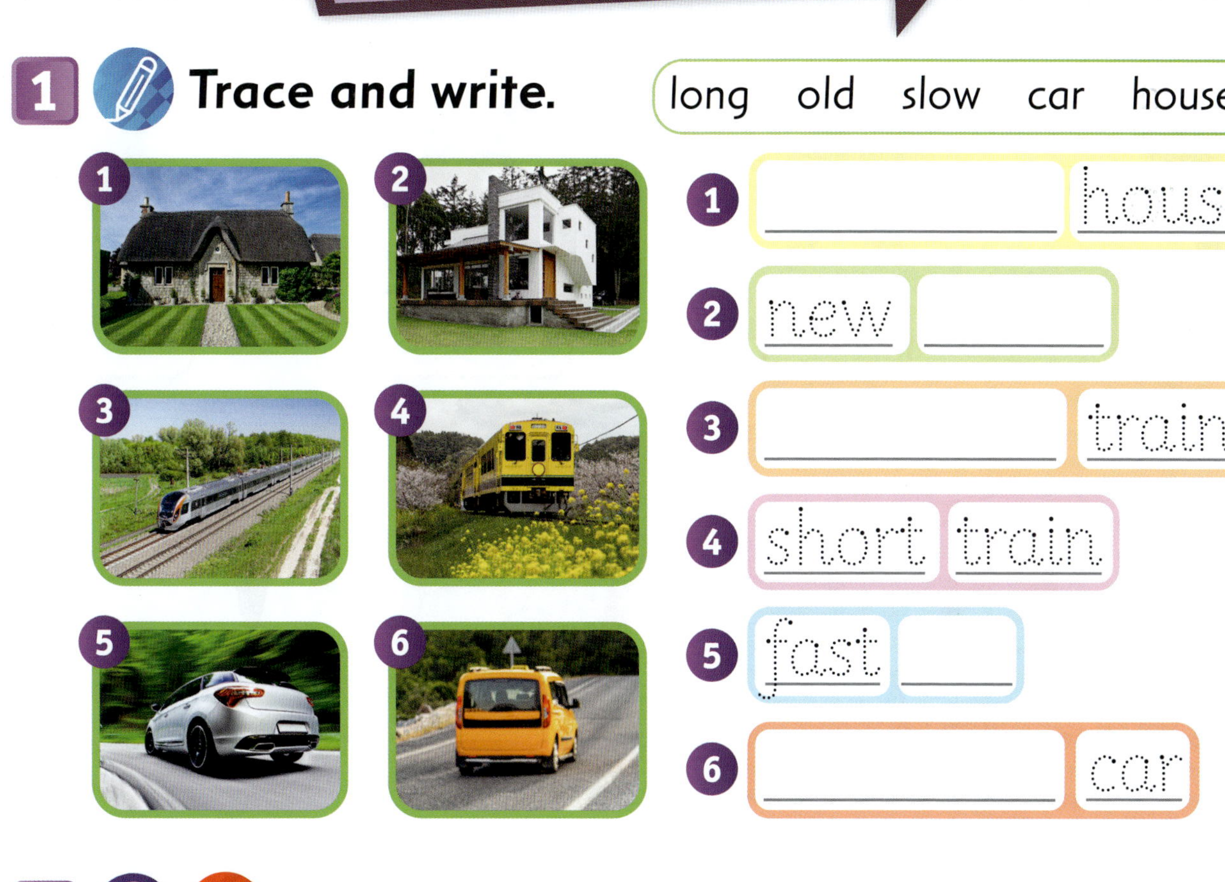

2 🎧 9.14 💬 **Listen and find. Then say.**

3 💡 🖊 **Think and color. Then stick!**

  **1** Listen and point. **2**   Trace and say.

black

blue

brown

green

orange

pink

purple

red

white

yellow

 Look and say the colors.

1

1 🎧 10.2 **Listen and point.**   **2** ✏️ 💬 **Trace and say.**

1
one

2
two

3
three

4
four

5
five

6
six

✏️ **Look, count, and circle.**

2

3

4

1  **Listen and point.**   **2**   **Trace and say.**

bed   chair

desk   poster

ball

kite

puppet

scooter

teddy bear

yo-yo

Look and say.

3

 Look and count chairs and backpacks. Write.

head

hand

arm

nose

leg

body

clap

shake

stomp

touch

 **Circle and count noses.**

1   **Listen and point.** **2**    **Trace and say.**

pants

skirt

shoes

socks

coat

dress

hat

scarf

sweater

T-shirt

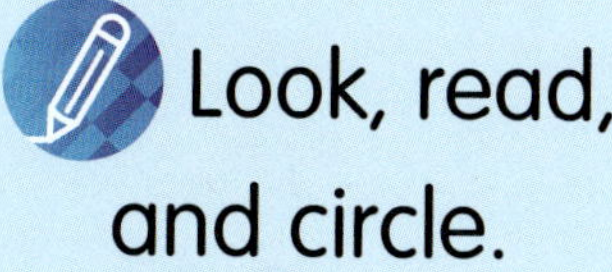 **Look, read, and circle.**

pants / skirt

scarf / shoes

6

1   **Listen and point.**   **2**   **Trace and say.**

ant   beetle   butterfly   ladybug

flower   mushroom   pond

river   rock   tree

 **Read, look, and circle.**

ant

apples

cake

soup

tea

cookies

ice cream

juice

noodles

pizza

sandwiches

✏️ 💬 **Look and trace. Then say** 🙂 **or** ☹️ **for you.**

soup   tea   juice

  **1**  Listen and point. **2**   **Trace and say.**

 What can zebras do?
Read and check (✔).

| walk ○ | run ○ | climb ○ |
| swim ○ | fly ○ | |

9

1   **Listen and point.** **2**    **Trace and say.**

car

house

street

train

fast

slow

long

short

old

new

 **Read and match.**

new		slow
fast		short
long		old

Alphabet

Aa ant

Ee elephant

Ff fox

Gg girl

Kk king

Ll lion

Mm monster

Qq queen

Rr rabbit

Ss skirt

Ww walk

Xx xylophone

Yy yellow

Bb

bird

Cc

cake

Dd

dinosaur

Hh

head

Ii

insect

Jj

jump

Nn

nose

Oo

orange

Pp

purple

Tt

tea

Uu

up

Vv

vulture

Zz

zebra

Pearson Education Limited
KAO Two
KAO Park
Hockham Way
Harlow, Essex
CM17 9SR
England
and Associated Companies throughout the world.

pearson.com/languages
© Pearson Education Limited 2022

First published 2022
Third impression 2024
ISBN: 978-1-292-44159-7
Set in Arta Medium 21/28pt

Printed in Slovakia by Neografia

Acknowledgements
The publishers and author would like to thank the following people for their feedback and comments during the development of the material: Dilek Akin, Burcu Hasbay, Martha Illescas, Maja Jankovic, Sandy Meza, Monica Medina, Olga Mokrushina, Soledad O'Keefe, Anita Parlaj.

Image Credits
123RF.com: Ababaka 55, Agencyby 47, Anna Trefilova 52, 105, Asife 75, Belchonock 22, 102, Christian Schnoor 88, Davide Guidolin 88, Dmitry Lobanov 65, 65, Erstudiostok 25, Gelpi 42, Happymay 62, 106, Jacek Chabraszewski 42, 82, 104, Jacob Laugesen 12, Kirill Ryzhov 17, Iacheev 37, Marctran 97, Martin Lisner 88, Mishoo 37, Oleksii Lukin 78, Olga Yastremska 52, 58, 105, Parinya Agsararattananont 57, Parinya Binsuk 25, Pavel Losevsky 67, Phasin Sudjai 45, Photoallel 58, Photomelon 22, 102, Pixelrobot 22, 102, Piyawat Nandeenopparit 96, Romangorielov 55, Ruslan Kudrin 58, Samuel Sequeira 52, 105, Sasi Ponchaisang 97, Sayfutdinov 15, Serezniy 27, Srapulsar38 39, 103, Stuart Porter 82, 108, Thomas Gowanlock 58, Vejaa 27, Vitalily73 52, 105; **Getty Images:** Ariel Skelley 57, Armin Staudt / EyeEm 39, 103, Caziopeia 72, 107, Christopher Hope-Fitch 37, Daniel Kaesler / EyeEm 26, Denise Crew 18, Domin_domin 52, 105, Emholk 47, FatCamera 43, FredFroese 36, Hakase_ 87, Iurii Garmash 92, 99, 109, Jade Albert Studio, Inc. 16, Jallfree 16, James Hager / robertharding 82, 108, Jaroon 46, JBryson 66, 95, Jose Luis Pelaez Inc 85, 96, Juanmonino 72, 107, Kei Kobayashi / EyeEm 88, Kirin_photo 17, Krisikorn Tanrattanakunl / EyeEm 36, Marin Tomas 92, 99, 109, Martin Ruegner 62, 106, Maurizio Siani 27, Michael Marsh/stocks photography/Getty images 68, Milan_Jovic 98, Nastasic 37, Nata_Snow 37, Nisha Sharma / EyeEm 18, Peter Dazeley 57, Picture by Tambako the Jaguar 88, Pinstock 27, Rastko Belic / EyeEm 22, 102, RazoomGames 17, Rubberball/Nicole Hill 97, Stretch Photography 77, Tagphoto 78, Thatsaphon Saengnarongrat / EyeEm 86, Westend61 78; **Pearson Education Ltd:** COLEMAN YUEN 62, 106, JULES SELMES 42, 67, 67, 85, 104, RAFAL TRUBISZ / PEARSON CENTRAL EUROPE SP. Z.O.O 26, TREVOR CLIFFORD 82; **Shutterstock:** 2347286 62, 106, A3pfamily 17, Achkin 61, 106, Africa Studio 12, 19, 101, Aksenova Natalya 107, Anatoliy Karlyuk 45, Andrea Slatter 35, ANDREI_SITURN 87, Andrey Burstein 17, Andrii Velykyi 75, ArtMediaFactory 88, B Calkins 88, Bmaki 22, 102, Danny Smythe 72, 107, Dmitrijs Mihejevs 88, Dmitry Lobanov 42, 104, Evgeny Karandaev 107, George Filyagin 32, 103, Here 56, Herjua 57, Irin-k 68, Jareerat 88, Jasper Suijten 62, 106, Jihan Nafiaa Zahri 95, Jim Barber 98, Karkas 52, 105, Kriangkrainetnangrong 82, 108, L Julia 46, LeNi 72, 107, Leonid Andronov 92, 99, 109, Lopolo 56, Loskutnikov 58, Lucie Lang 39, 103, Ludmila Ivashchenko 58,

Luis Molinero 5, Lukas Gojda 32, 103, Lunatictm 39, 103, Mai Groves 5, Marharyta Gangalo 76, Martina_L 52, 105, MIA Studio 66, Mikhail Turov 52, 105, MNStudio 87, Morrowind 35, Mubus7 92, 99, 109, Nataly Studio 107, Netrun78 47, Nexus 7 72, 88, 107, Nikshor 39, 103, Novak.elcic 62, 106, Oksana2010 107, Olga Sapegina 42, 104, Palto 61, 106, Patrick Foto 61, 106, Pavel L Photo and Video 67, Photographee.eu 28, Pixel-Shot 39, 103, PV productions 87, 98, Robert Kneschke 77, ROMANO NICOLA 61, 106, Ruslan Kudrin 52, 105, Santiago Cornejo 92, 99, 109, Sergey Novikov 9, Sergiy1975 22, 102, SergiyN 82, Shippee 17, Stockcreations 72, 107, Subbotina Anna 47, Sunny Forest 47, Tamapapat 92, 99, 109, Tom Wang 76, Tosaphon C 82, 108, TTphoto 82, 108, TY Lim 15, Valentyn Volkov 78, Valerii_M 49, Wavebreakmedia 37, Xiaorui 52, Yellow Cat 32, 103, Yuganov Konstantin 9, Yuliia D 86, Zelfit 98.

Illustrations
Emily Cooksey/Plum Pudding pp.93 (kid art); **Cristina de Iera/Plum Pudding** pp. 16, 21 (backpack), 24, 32 (rubric spots), 44, 60, 64, 70, 72, 73, 74, 76, 84, 86, 90, 94; **Anna-Lena Kuehler/Plum Pudding** pp. 11, 13, 21, 27, 42, 45, 47, 57, 77, 97; **Emma Randall/Plum Pudding (course characters)**; **Sam Rennocks/Advocate** pp.26, 62, 63, 66, 68, 83, 84; **Christos Skaltsas/Advocate** (cutouts), pp. 18, 22, 23, 26 (Ex 3), 29, 32 (Ex 2), 33, 34, 43, 53, 54, 58, 62 (Ex 2 mushroom), 66 (Ex 3), 78, 79, 86, 92, 94, 96, 98; **Abi Tompkins/Plum Pudding** (doodles); **Hannah Wood/Advocate** pp.28, 32 (Ex 3), 36, 52, 93.

Unit 1

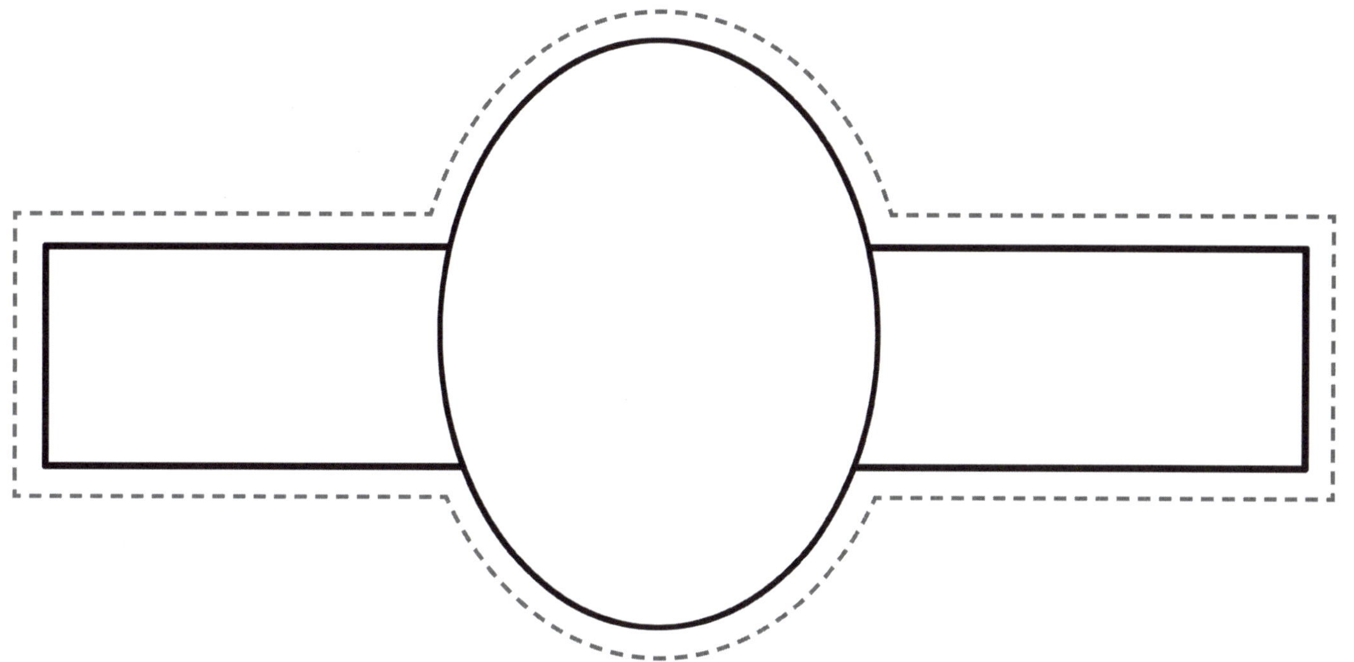

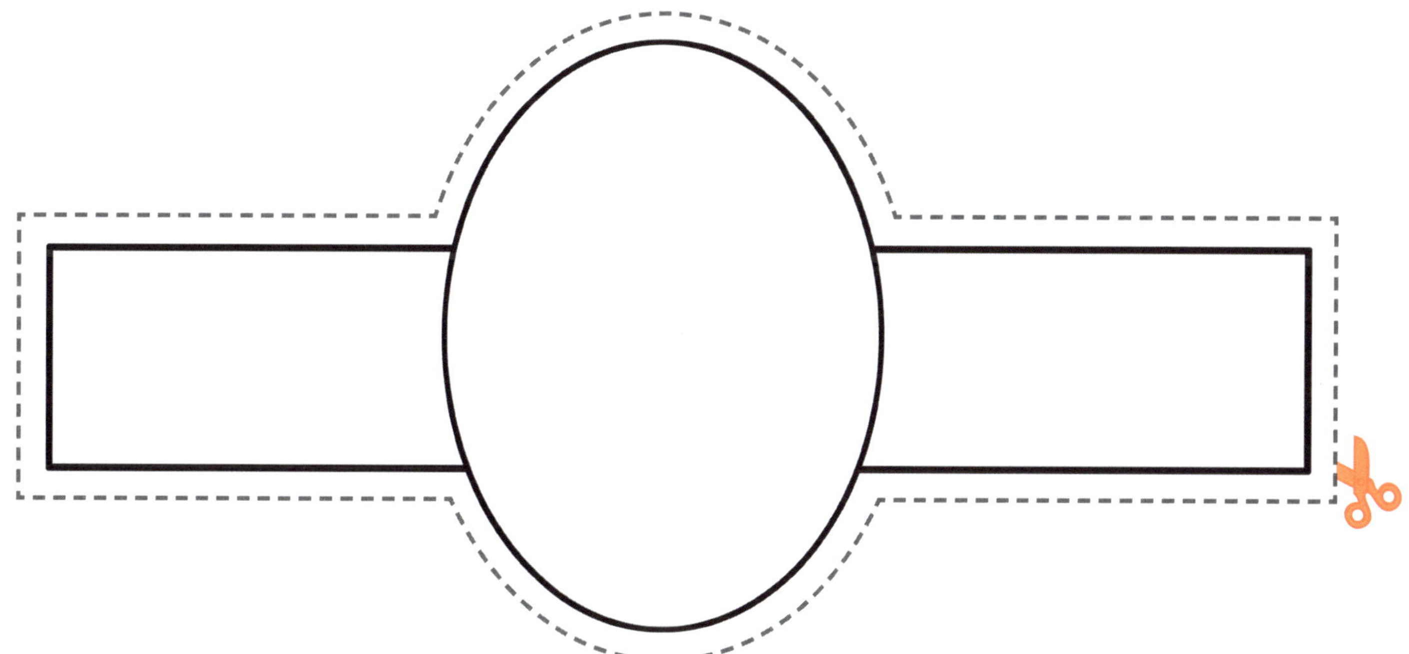

Unit 2

Unit 3

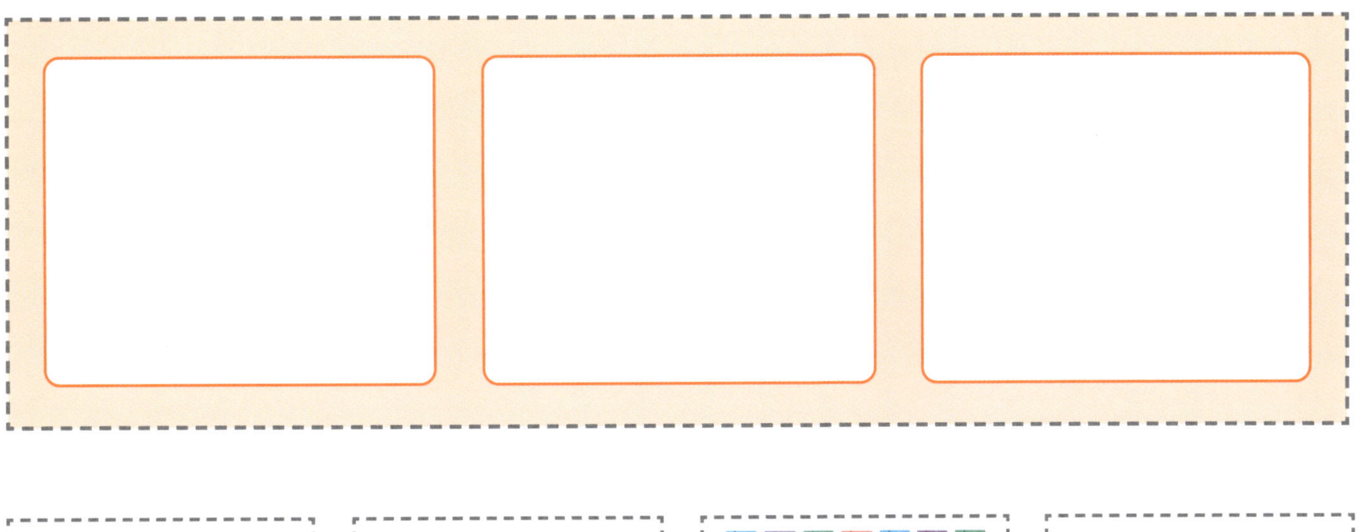

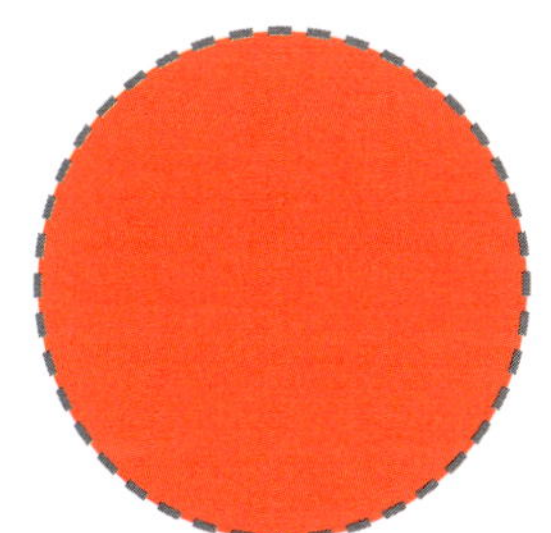

Unit 4

Key: fold line

Unit 5

Unit 6

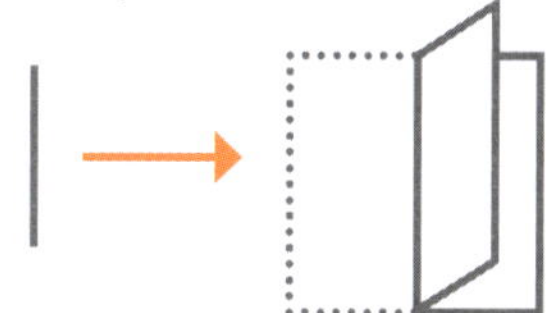

Unit 7

Unit 8

Unit 9

Welcome

Unit 1

Unit 2

Unit 3

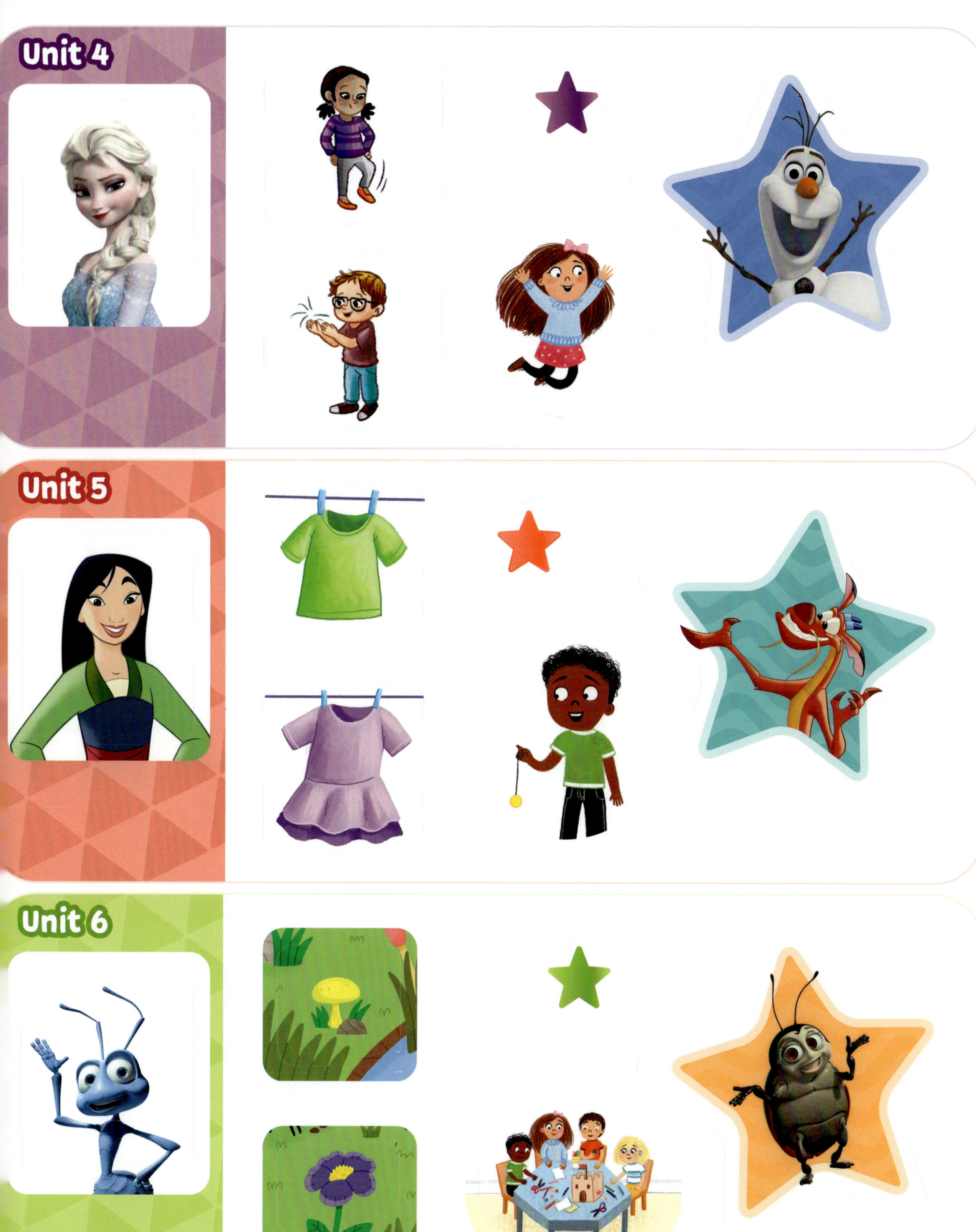

Unit 4

Unit 5

Unit 6